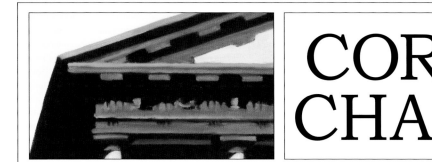
CORNICES OF CHARLESTON

PAINTINGS BY *Susan Romaine*
PHOTOGRAPHS BY *Jack Alterman*

INTRODUCTION BY *John Caroll Doyle*
FOREWORD BY *Harlan Greene*

We gratefully acknowledge the unsung artisans in our lives who helped us to publish this book, giving their time (and giving up their time with us), their encouragement, and their talent.

Photographs copyright © Jack Alterman
Paintings copyright © Susan Romaine

ISBN 0-9767171-1-5
LCCN 2005924517

Book Design by Steve Lepre of Sunhead Projects, LLC
Printed by Jostens Charlotte, NC USA

INTRODUCTION

By John Caroll Doyle

In the tradition of the royal court artist, Jack Alterman and Susan Romaine have employed their talents in photography and paint to present us with portraits of a forgotten side of Charleston's architectural nobility.

Some of Charleston's most noble buildings, crowned with regal cornices, have agreed to "sit" for Jack and Susan, knowing that these two artists understand and value their noble bloodline. This bloodline reaches back to those who gave birth to the splendid structures: architects, artisans, and common labourers, both black and white, including Europeans and workers from the far corners of the Mediterranean.

As we turn the pages of this enchanting collection of pictures, we can begin to truly see, maybe for the first time, the glory that has always loomed above us. In fact, for more years than most of us have lived, these giants in stone and brick have been looking down with watchful concern, as benevolent kings and queens watch over their subjects.

These regal buildings have witnessed parades celebrating Christmas, azaleas, and the return of war-weary young men. Boy scouts and girl scouts have stepped in time under their watchful gaze, and Shriners, behaving like court jesters, have scooted gleefully around in midget cars for their entertainment.

In the 1930's, movie houses, such as the Riviera, provided relief from emotional and economic depression with their musical fantasies and five handkerchief love stories.

Chase Furniture helped young couples furnish modest homes with beds and sofas on the "lay-a-way" plan.

On Broad Street, stately law offices housed attorneys who spoke for those who found it hard to speak for themselves.

Brides found their dream dresses at shops along King Street such as Rosalie Meyers' or Elza's.

Children felt the elation of speed and independence with bicycles from Robinson's Bicycle Shop on the corner of King and Ann Streets.

Bobbysoxers flirted and spun on chromed soda-fountain stools at Kress Department Store.

Music lovers whiled away afternoons listening to records in the booths at Siegling's Music House at Beaufain and King.

Although these majestic buildings and their festooned cornices have developed patina with age and changed hands many times, Jack Alterman and Susan Romaine have captured the love and glory that their builders originally envisioned.

Jack and Susan have given us a beautiful visual guide book to the streets of Charleston, in which true nobility can be seen. And maybe, just maybe, because of this book, Jack Alterman and Susan Romaine will help us to look up, to see how these wonderful works of art reflect our own nobility.

Thank you Jack; thank you Susan.

John Caroll Doyle, artist.

245 King Street
at the corner of Beaufain Street

FOREWORD

By Harlan Greene

Charleston is mostly a horizontal city.

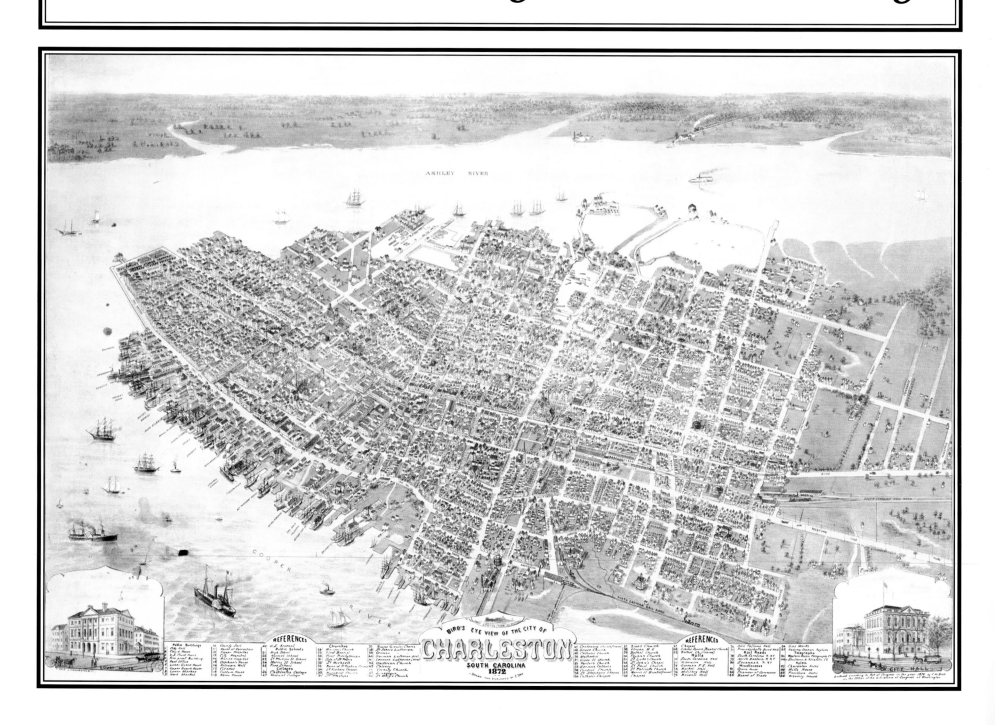

And that both apt and fitting. For – after all—it was the search for new horizons that drew the first settlers here from across the sea. And upon arriving, they took the grand flat unobstructed views to heart, incorporating those lines and layouts in their buildings. The houses they put up may seem to be vertical at first glance. The city's characteristic and distinctive "single" houses may appear to be tall and narrow from the street: but walk through a piazza door or enter the garden and the house's true nature appears: the rooms stretch along like box cars deep into the lot. The buildings in Charleston are longer than they are high; they parallel the shape of the peninsula itself – sticking like a finger out to sea.

Over the years, Charlestonians did put up a few tall buildings – churches mostly, so their spires punctuated the sky and drew attention to the place – not necessarily a good thing. Far out at sea, the steeples were like pointers, giving away the city's hiding place to the Spanish, some pirates, and the British and Union forces eventually. The tall spires of the town were used by the enemy to draw a bead on the city; St. Michael's steeple, the oldest and perhaps the most handsome in town, was painted black to keep it from catching the sun and being too helpful to the enemy.

Another enemy of the town has been heat; it rises; so it is hotter on the higher floors of buildings. And then there is the soil, too – soft and marshy. So much of the peninsula on which the city sits is actually landfill so that many buildings now look like the tower of Pisa as they've begun to lean and list. For these many reasons – and because there was enough space for a small population – Charlestonians kept a low profile, not building most structures higher than a palmetto tree. Piazzas only two or three stories high caught breezes, and their depth cut off the sun from entering the rooms. As late as 1857, when there were already a few buildings five and six stories high, Charleston was still a flat and horizontal place. William Gilmore Simms, the great Southern writer who made Charleston a cultural capital before the Civil War, wrote then of the city that, "It is built like Venice, upon flats. So low is the land, that the illusion that it is built directly upon the sea, continues until you approach quite near it. This illusion is productive of a picturesque effect, but not sufficient to compensate you for the relief which would be yielded by an elevated background, or by lofty eminences...." He clearly regretted the flatness of the low country and its buildings.

So for many reasons, Charlestonians did not develop the habit of looking up. Over the years, they looked forward with hope, and backwards with pride, but as sectional differences developed, they took to looking down on those who were different politically. Pride puffed up the city before the Civil War (and this might be another reason Charlestonians did not look up – imagine the horror if someone, other than God, might be looking down on you!) This pride, of course, precipitated a fall. With the economic depression that resulted in 1865 at the loss of the Civil War, the city was poor for generations; even those with money had little desire to follow the prevailing heights of fashion of the day. Charleston liked the old ways – Greek temples of classic proportions, single houses, with porches (or "piazzas") on everything. It became a point of pride that the city kept its historic skyline, looking eighteenth or early nineteenth century in its outer and inner worldviews. As if in warning, the earthquake of 1886 took aim at those buildings and the parts of them that stuck up higher: steeples and parapets toppled, and nearly every chimney fell in the city.

The death knell for the horizontality of Charleston came in 1911 with the construction of the People's Building. Residents were shocked when a "skyscraper" of seven stories towered above Broad Street, and they did not like the idea of a bank jockeying with God's churches for supremacy, plunging neighbors into chilly grim shadows of things to come. Charleston started to protect itself in 1931 with preservation laws; height soon became an issue, as more and more tall buildings were thrown up, destroying the skyline of the early city. Over the years numerous grass-roots groups sprang up to fight high rises and the threat of tall buildings literally overshadowing the low-slung city. So, the refusal to see virtue in high places continued, often for more obvious reasons too: pedestrians and drivers have to keep their eyes down to navigate around the flagstone walks, eccentric curbs, bumpy brick and cobblestone streets of the city.

It's a shame really that we've not been looking up all these years, for dancing above our heads, are strange and wonderful things: elaborate cornices, rising Egyptian suns, names and dates of the vainglorious departed, the faces of stoic, all-seeing ladies, the city's seal. There are steeples winking in accord, while below folks think they are going their separate ways as they enter different church doorways. Faces grin and leer. Swags decorate, egg and dart border the sky, and urns sprout greenery. Fire towers that once rang out hurricane warnings now rust silently; and communication towers stare at steeples, in duets of different types of communicating.

Like books no one reads or movies no one sees, these scenes present themselves to no audiences, going on in their lonely existences, unsuspected, unknown, showing themselves only to the gulls, the air, eternity. There is a whole other world up there, up above our heads, above the streets and curbs, our gates and gardens and doorways.

And like the world of old Charleston, like those gates and gardens and doors, these cornices and gables and glories are disappearing. Many are suffering the same fate of the great statue of Charity that once topped the Orphan House, once one of Charleston's tallest buildings. It and the building it graced received no mercy: she fell ignominiously to lay face down in the dirt for a generation.

And we have been losing other heaven-reaching virtues, too, besides Charity. Details are vanishing off the tops of buildings, falling to effects of storm and wind, rot and decay and the homogenizing process and standardization of more recent centuries. It is more than brick and stone and plaster and alabaster that we are losing, more than just the embellishment of architects, often the piece de resistance, like a finial on a tureen, acting as the final grace note on an object of beauty. For up here, among the rooftops, are shouted declarations and cries in the wind - dates and names of the builders who laid claim to posterity – newer Greek and Jewish immigrants too late to have streets named for them, but who nevertheless

wanted to add their names to the chorus of those who shaped the city. Here, too, as if in mime, are clues to the origins of some structures – why else would a bicycle ride the sky or a business emblazon its cornice with two dates from two different centuries? In these architectural details our predecessors attempted to grasp and render beauty as well as give meaning. In the process, as they made their declarations against the sky, there came intersections of the moment and eternity, as taste met time, and fashion usurped utility. Looking up, you can see the seams of time where a new façade joins an old structure, and discern how humble structures have put on false fronts of pomposity, as well as the way follies of design mask a time worn integrity. These and other details are not extraneous, but are part of the soul and sinew of the buildings – and the city. For what are buildings but the vessels in which we launch our beliefs and dreams? And their elaborate decorations –are they not our vanities? And what about all the attention to detail, and doing things right, no matter if anyone will see them? Aren't these skills and virtues just as in danger of disappearing as the designs they embody on the tops of buildings? It's something like Braille up there – against the sky are messages of our mortality and dreams.

This drama going on above our heads, unglimpsed before, is now ours. For Jack Alterman and Susan Romaine, in this book of photographs and paintings, have literally lifted us up and given us entry to a world we ignored, a world simultaneously old and unseen, but also exciting and new. They give us not just a bird's eye view, but a totally different way to examine our world. And this is fitting as well, for it is exactly what we expect our great artists to do.

And they have done it so thrillingly that one has to give up words; prose falters as the images come into view. Neighborhood by neighborhood, and street by street, here is a Charleston we have never known, or have had to crane our necks and lift our eyes against the sun to see. Flipping these pages, one gets the feeling of almost taking wing. These artists allow us to expand our horizons, take off and join in the aerial ballet of design and time going on atop the cornices of Charleston's buildings.

THE GARDEN THEATRE
371 King Street

MEETING STREET
Broad Street to Calhoun Street

BROAD STREET
Meeting Street to East Bay Street

LOWER EAST BAY
Queen Street to South Battery

Broad Street & St. Michael's Church between East Bay & Meeting Streets
BROAD STREET I
40" x 40" ~ oil on canvas

FOUR CORNERS OF LAW
Post Office, County Courthouse
Broad & Meeting Streets

Four Corners of Law
City Hall, St. Michael's Church
Broad & Meeting Streets

Broad Street from Church Street to State Street

46 Broad Street
with St. Philip's Steeple

CONFEDERATE HOME
60 - 64 Broad Street

15 & 17 Broad Street

The Exchange Building to 17 Broad Street
BROAD STREET II
40" x 40" ~ oil on canvas

Top of 11 Broad Street

9 Broad Street

141 East Bay Street

*1 Broad Street
at East Bay Street*
MORNING ON EAST BAY
18" x 14" ~ oil on canvas

29 East Battery

NEXT PAGE
Circular Congregational Church (center);
The Gibbes Museum of Art (right);
St. Michael's steeple in the distance
THREE MONTH WINDOW
24" x 48" ~ oil on canvas

LEFT
161 East Bay Street & St. Philip's steeple

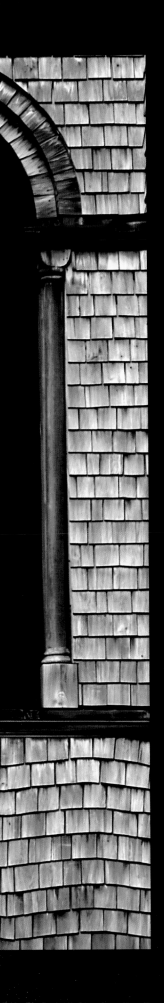

Circular Congregational Church & St. Philip's steeple
150 Meeting Street

Gibbes Museum of Art
135 Meeting Street

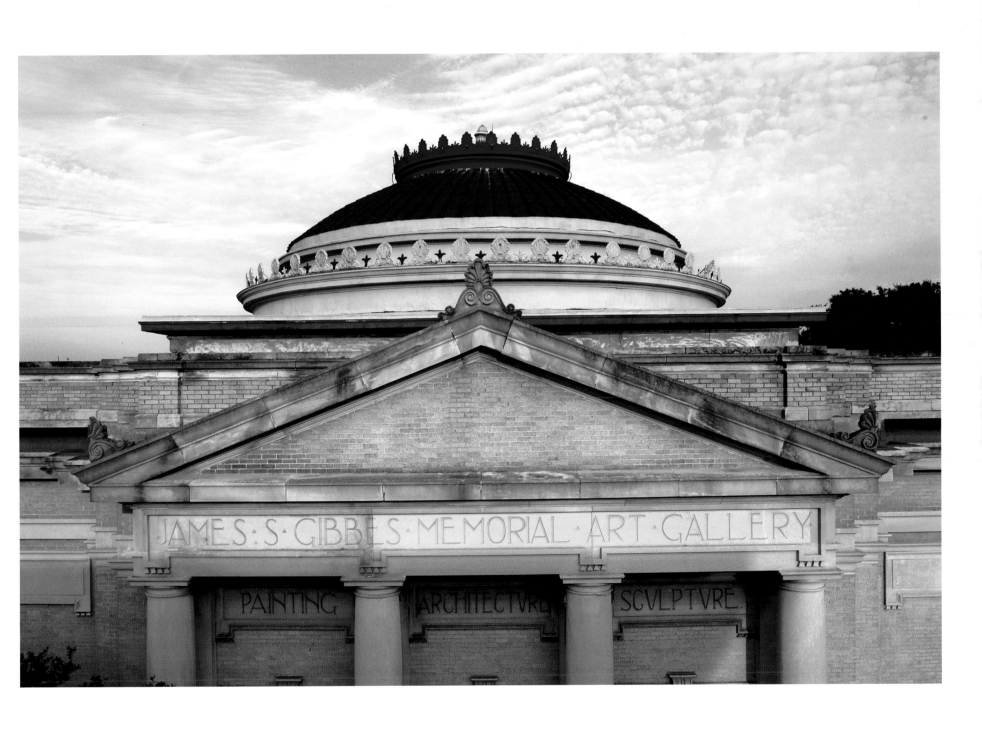

Gibbes Museum of Art Dome

188 Meeting Street
MEETING AT MARKET
16" x 12" ~ oil on linen

Market Hall, 188 Meeting Street

309 Meeting Street & statue of John C. Calhoun

LOWER KING STREET

Broad Street to Calhoun Street

Intersection of King & Calhoun Streets; looking South

158 ~ 160 King Street

202 King Street

208 & 206 King Street

212 & 208 King Street
14" x 11" ~ oil on linen

King Street at Horlbeck Alley
188 ~ 190 KING
24" x 18" ~ oil on linen

Majestic Square
Corner of King & Market Streets

The Riveria Theatre
227 King Street

243 King Street
at the corner of Beaufain Street

King Street at Wentworth Street looking South;
St. Michael's steeple in the distance

Southwest Corner of
King & Wentworth Streets
MORNING ON KING
24" x 18" ~ oil on canvas

KRESS BUILDING
King Street looking North; near Society Street

King Street near Burns Lane;
looking South

King Street, South of Burns Lane
LOWER KING
36" x 36" ~ oil on canvas

King Street, South of George Street
316 ~ 314 KING
14" x 18" ~ oil on linen

West side of King Street, at Calhoun Street

Northeast corner of
King & George Streets

Southwest corner of King & Calhoun Streets
CALHOUN AND KING
16" x 20" ~ oil on linen

UPPER KING STREET

Calhoun Street to Columbus Street

Cannon Street near King Street
CANNON STREET FIRE STATION
14" x 18" ~ oil on linen

THE FRANCIS MARION HOTEL
Northwest corner of King & Calhoun Streets

414 King Street

440 & 438 King
24" x 18" ~ oil on linen

445 King Street with St. Patrick's steeple

507 King Street

493 & 495 King Street,
with St. Patrick's steeple

476 & 474 King
12" x 16" ~ oil on linen

SCHWINN ON BASIL
18" x 14" ~ oil on linen

Corner of King and Ann Streets

513 ~ 515 King Street,
with Central Baptist's steeple

MORRIS AND KING
18" x 24" ~ oil on linen

MARY AND KING
18" x 24" ~ oil on linen

496 King Street (foreground), 517 King Street

KING AND MARY
28" x 48" ~ oil on linen

BLUESTEIN'S
20" x 16" ~ oil on linen

510 & 502 King Street

545, 547 & 549 King Street

545, 547 & 549 King
12" x 16" ~ oil on linen

565 King Street,
with Cannon Street Fire Tower

557, 557 1/2 & 559 KING
9" x 12" ~ oil on linen

556 King
14" x 11" ~ oil on linen

577 & 579 King Street

UPPER KING TO READ'S
18" x 24" ~ oil on linen

593 King Street,
at Spring Street

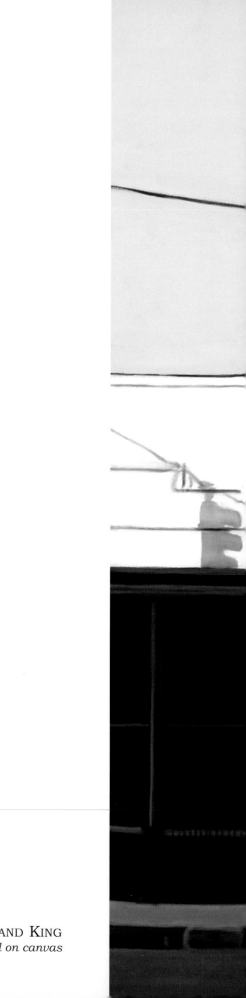

COLUMBUS AND KING
30" x 40" ~ oil on canvas

Susan Romaine

One clear winter morning I took a walk along King Street and happened to look up. The sight took my breath away. I saw the cornices of Charleston for what seemed like the first time. Sunlight poured over rounded surfaces and sharp edges and etched their strong geometric shapes in shadow and color against an intensely blue sky - each cornice claiming the unique time and space in which it was built. The 1950's next to 1800, beside Neo-classic, Victorian, Federal, Art Deco, 1980 – all within a morning's walk.

It wasn't until I was nearly finished with the paintings for my first "Cornices of Charleston" show, that I realized many more than just these images needed to be captured, not only on canvas but also in a book. Every cornice, however, did not make a painting. To allow many to revel in their breadth and beauty, to see what I had seen when I finally looked up, a book would need artfully rendered photographs. I turned to my friend, Jack Alterman, and asked if he would be interested in collaborating. I knew this talented and creative photographer would lend his own unique voice to the book. His photographs capture far more than I had ever imagined they would, lending a fullness and beauty that could not have been achieved by my paintings alone. It was also with Jack's help that we were able to recruit Harlan Greene, John Doyle and Steve Lepre onto our "dream team", each lending his voice to our tribute to the unsung artisans who had written Charleston's history so eloquently across the sky.

In the beginning, I simply had to paint Charleston's cornices to capture what I had felt that clear winter morning. In the end, this project became far greater than the sum of the parts we all played in its creation.

"JACK" 20" X 16" OIL ON CANVAS

Jack Alterman

This project was about finding a new perspective on familiar places. It was about two fine art forms, photography and painting, standing next to each other with a small degree of separation. It was an adventure.

We all know about the magical times of twilight and dusk. Those times when the light points out to us the textures and details of everything we see. During these short moments of the day, in June and again in December, I took my new perspective and found a wealth of familiar places.

The tools of my craft were not unusual. I used 35mm cameras, both film and digital and sometimes a larger 2 1/4 format. What was different was my platform. A 45 foot Cherry Picker. It was like having a magic carpet to explore the many new vantage points of the city. From this mechanical balcony I photographed the most private yet most exposed details. I watched the early morning sunlight as it slowly painted color on the cornices and facades of the buildings. From my loft I quietly listened as the city came to life below me.

Later, in the afternoon, I returned to watch the second act play out the day. The curtain rose with the setting sun revealing the opposite side of the street and more of the marvelous art that was created so long ago. There was the story just in front of me and then the layers of the city beyond. Finally, I watched the sunlight fade and the lights of the city begin to glow. I parked the beast and walked home eager to begin again in the morning.

Like Susan, I had found my new perspective and will not take familiar places for granted again.

Fig. 2.

9¾
9¾

1 in 5¼

1.5

1. 5. 05
1. 5. 5
1. 5. 834
1. 4.75
1. 4. 6

1. 4. 694   11.3   9.5
.25   10. 5
10. 234

9 .366

9. 275

8. 1

1. 1.

4

4

Fig. 1.

1. 160